I KNOW OVER AND UNDER

By Rosie Banks

Gareth Stevens
PUBLISHING

first concepts

Directions can
tell us where.

Over and under
are directions.

The hand is
over the car.

The hand is
under the car.

People walk
over the bridge.

11

People walk
under the bridge.

The cat goes
over the fence.

15

The cat goes
under the fence.

17

The ball is
over her head.

The ball is
under her foot.

21

We can go
over and under too!

Please visit our website, www.garethstevens.com. For a free color catalog of all our high-quality books, call toll free 1-800-542-2595 or fax 1-877-542-2596.

Library of Congress Cataloging-in-Publication Data
Names: Banks, Rosie, 1978- author.
Title: I know over and under / Rosie Banks.
Description: New York : Gareth Stevens Publishing, [2023] | Series: I know directions
Identifiers: LCCN 2022024816 (print) | LCCN 2022024817 (ebook) | ISBN 9781538282939 (library binding) | ISBN 9781538282915 (paperback) | ISBN 9781538282946 (ebook)
Subjects: LCSH: Orientation–Juvenile literature. | Space perception–Juvenile literature.
Classification: LCC BF299.O7 B364 2023 (print) | LCC BF299.O7 (ebook) | DDC 152.14/2–dc23/eng/20220720
LC record available at https://lccn.loc.gov/2022024816
LC ebook record available at https://lccn.loc.gov/2022024817

First Edition

Published in 2023 by
Gareth Stevens Publishing
2544 Clinton Street
Buffalo, NY 14224

Copyright © 2023 Gareth Stevens Publishing

Designer: Leslie Taylor
Editor: Therese Shea

Photo credits: Cover, p. 1 (stripes) Eky Studio/Shutterstock.com, (image) Damsea/Shutterstock.com; p. 3 Mimadeo/Shutterstock.com; p. 5 Captain Wang/Shutterstock.com; p. 7 New Africa/Shutterstock.com; p. 9 Peerayot/Shutterstock.com; p. 11 Cliff Day/Shutterstock.com; p. 13 Peter_Fleming/Shutterstock.com; p. 15 Katho Menden/Shutterstock.com; p. 17 Andi111/Shutterstock.com; p. 19 Eric Eric/Shutterstock.com; p. 21 Dmitry Lobanov/Shutterstock.com; p. 23 Monkey Business Images/Shutterstock.com.

Printed in the United States of America

CPSIA compliance information: Batch #CWGS23: For further information contact Gareth Stevens at 1-800-542-2595.